COFFEE

Stefanie "Sparrow" Kelley-McNease

Copyright © 2025 by Stefanie "Sparrow" Kelley-McNease

All rights reserved. No part of this book may be used or reproduced by any means, graphic, electronic, or mechanical, including photocopying, recording, taping, or by any information storage retrieval system, without the written permission of the publisher except in the case of brief quotations embodied in critical articles and reviews.

Dedication

To my mom and dad who instilled positivity in me, to go after every goal I set, and to keep God as the forefront of everything. To my husband, you have increased my desire to do more because we both want more, for that I love you. To Brit, Sonya, and Deidre thank you for encouraging me to create this book of quotes, you gave me the key to ignite another gift I did not know needed a start! To my family and friends that support everything I do, your loyalty is greater than anything, this book is also dedicated to you.

Your greatest moment of wisdom
comes from your greatest
moment of mistake.

The sky isn't the limit when there's still a universe to reach.

You have to drop your wish
so your hands are free to catch
your dream.

God cannot redeem your regrets
unless you release them!
Release your regrets so God can
provide your redemption.

When you're driving towards your goal, there will be detours, roadblocks, traffic, and even unexpected curves. But no matter what is in front of you...never let up on the gas. Keep driving to your goal.

A new miracle can't be received with an old mindset.

Don't let the insecurities of your past prevent you from securing your future.

Speak *nothing is impossible* language; think *nothing is impossible* thoughts.

There is no expiration date on your purpose nor your destiny.

Customize your prayer and
strategize your obedience.

Happiness is your own job! Never search for someone to do that job, because if you do, you will place your happiness in someone else's hands.

Never be afraid of going slowly.
Be afraid of standing still.

Defeat is a choice, and since you *have* choices...choose not to be defeated.

When you're destined to fly high, you're also destined for turbulence! Remember *Who* your *Pilot* is (God).... with *Him* you *will* make it to your destination.

Don't allow people to determine
how God is to you!
Or who He is to you!

A test and trial are nothing
but a preparation for a promotion
from God!

Some storms come to make you weak before they make you strong. Sometimes you must be stripped of everything, like a twister, to be rebuilt from the ground up.

To go after the B.I.G. you must
   (B)ring
   (I)n
   (G)od

Master the skill to have
   (F)earless
   (O)ptimism of one's
   (C)ourse
   (U)ntil
   (S)uccessful

God will not release anything
you don't ask for.

P.U.S.H.
Pray Until Something Happens.

Forgiveness doesn't make you weak. Forgiveness doesn't mean you forgot.

Never rush time
and never waste time.

God will evict certain
things and people from
your life to place
the right people in your life.

Know facts before you allow a circumstance to create fiction.

Proper preparation prevents
poor performance.

How you enter a room determines how you're interpreted.

Remember God is *the source,* not the resource.

When you forgave the person,
you must also forgive the offense.

Walk in your own purpose...
Don't chase after one because you
desire someone else's.

A heart can't be broken if you never give it to be dropped.

Hate it
so you can change it.

Three Habits of a Healthy Heart
1. Know what to hate.
2. Know where to hide.
(Psalms 119:114)
3. Know how to have hope.

Raise your standards but
lower your tolerance.

Prayer should not be your last resort, but your first instinct.

The most significant thing you
can do when you start your day
is to intentionally worship
God and pray.

Give God flex space. Space to flex, grow, and stretch you past your mental capability!

What you desire greatly can become delayed greatly, but that's when you must trust God greater.

Whenever you have a vision or a plan, it's like a train with no tracks and no direction. You're the conductor of a powerful engine that can only move once the tracks are placed and the GPS is activated. But when you give that plan, that vision to God...he will not only provide the train tracks, but the direction. He is the GPS, the guide to our plans.

Define who you are by what you conquered, not by what or who stood against you.

Acknowledge the accomplishment *first*, then set the next goal. If you don't stop and acknowledge the progress, you'll never appreciate the success.

You are the architect of either your own destruction or your own construction.

If there's a solution to it,
then it's not a problem.

Never let the things you want
make you forget the things
you have!

Frustrations can produce fruits.

Influence doesn't require popularity. You can be impactful without being popular (Hebrews 13:5).

Anything that pulls you from your authenticity is not best for you. If you must change or conform what is authentic in you, it's not the real you.

Be careful of thoughts you allow
your heart to digest.

In some seasons, God will reduce you, so he can refill you with what he has destined for you.

It's never too late for God, no matter how bad the situation is.

God is not going to check your schedule to do his will.

Prioritize what is important to *you*.

You must unlearn old things to learn and develop new things.

Never despise small beginnings.
Those small beginnings can lead
to something big!

You have to *speak* what you want to see! God has given you the authority to do so! (Luke 10:19, Proverbs 18:21)

Remember your strength is like
hair: it can be cut,
but it will grow back!

You must hate the things you want to detach from.

You will miss what *is* when you stay stuck in what *was*.

If you have a goal, set a date to accomplish it. Otherwise, it'll just be a wish.

You must see victory
to seize victory.

The gift is in the *middle*.
The goal is in the *middle*.
The miracle is in the *middle*.

I will not *labor* in something
God is not *building*.

Stay low but aim high.

Happiness is a journey,
not a stop at a destination.

You can't properly strategize
if you're constantly scared.

Anything you consistently practice
you will become good at.
That includes bad habits.

It is difficult to grow what
God didn't plant in you.

Use failure as a fertilizer to plant ambition that will grow your future.

When you focus on
what's not happening,
you don't see what
God is making happen.

Worry is a down payment
on a problem you're not meant to have.

You don't need permission to be great.

It only takes one match to burn
a haystack and one fire to ignite a mind.

www.ingramcontent.com/pod-product-compliance
Lightning Source LLC
LaVergne TN
LVHW051035070526
838201LV00009B/200